THE
SEQUENCE
TO
SUCCESS

STUDY GUIDE

Scripture quotations marked KJV are taken from the King James Version of the Bible. Public domain. Scripture quotations marked NIV are taken from the Holy Bible, New International Version®, NIV®. Copyright © 1973, 1978, 1984, 2011 by Biblica, Inc.™ Used by permission of Zondervan. All rights reserved worldwide. www.zondervan.com. The "NIV" and "New International Version" are trademarks registered in the United States Patent and Trademark Office by Biblica, Inc.™ | Scripture quotations marked NKJV are taken from the New King James Version®. Copyright © 1982 by Thomas Nelson. Used by permission. All rights reserved. | Scripture quotations marked TLB are taken from The Living Bible copy- right © 1971 by Tyndale House Foundation. Used by permission of Tyndale House Publishers Inc., Carol Stream, Illinois 60188. All rights reserved. The Living Bible, TLB, and The Living Bible logo are registered trademarks of Tyndale House Publishers. | Scripture quotations marked NLT are taken from the Holy Bible, New Living Translation, copyright © 1996, 2004, 2015 by Tyndale House Foundation. Used by permission of Tyndale House Publishers, Inc., Carol Stream, Il-linois 60188. All rights reserved. | Scripture quotations marked MSG are taken from THE MESSAGE, copyright © 1993, 1994, 1995, 1996, 2000, 2001, 2002 by Eugene H. Peterson. Used by permission of NavPress. All rights reserved. Represented by Tyndale House Publishers, Inc. | Scripture quotations marked GNT are from the Good News Translation in Today's English Version—Second Edition. Copyright © 1992 by American Bible Society. Used by Permission.

For foreign and subsidiary rights, contact the author.

Interior Photos: © Shutterstock, Andrew van Tilborgh, Jessica Hegland, Dominic Fondon

ISBN: 9781950718399   1 2 3 4 5 6 7 8 9 10

Printed in the United States of America

THE
SEQUENCE
TO
SUCCESS

THREE O'S THAT WILL TAKE YOU
ANYWHERE IN LIFE

STUDY GUIDE
SAMUEL R. CHAND

AVAIL

CONTENTS

INTRODUCTION

How Did I Get Here?

o o o

BIG IDEA / The three-fold cycle of observations, opinions, and opportunities is essential for every single leader to understand. Only when we're cognizant of our subconscious ideas can we intentionally ensure that we're presenting ourselves, and recognizing others, in a way that's in line with our true potential.

READ / Introduction in *The Sequence to Success*

○ ○ ○

RESPOND /

In your own words, how would you differentiate an observation from an opinion?

_____

_____

_____

_____

_____

_____

REFLECT AND DISCUSS /

"Virtually all of us can trace our current situations back to three crucial engagements: someone *observed* us, formed a positive *opinion* of us, and then said, "I think you'd be good at. . . Let me give you this *opportunity*."

What are the top 5 opportunities you've been given in your life to date?

_____

_____

_____

_____

_____

What do you notice in Sam's story about the people who gave him an opportunity? What does their offer to Sam say about the way in which opportunities are created?

_____

_____

_____

_____

○ ○ ○

REFLECT AND DISCUSS /

"We react to our observation, but we seldom stop to analyse before we respond—it just happens and it happens immediately."

○ ○ ○

RESPOND /

Why do you think we form instantaneous opinions of people based on our observations?

_____

_____

_____

_____

According to Sam, why is it so important to be conscious of the observations and opinions we're forming—both for ourselves and for those around us?

_____

_____

_____

_____

Have you ever had someone recognize—or even reveal—a hidden talent inside of you? What was it, and how did this person speak into your life?

_____

_____

_____

_____

What's one skill or awareness you'd like to improve upon by the time you finish this study guide? Why is this competency important to you?

_____

_____

_____

_____

PART 1 / Observations

CHAPTER 1

The Camera is Always On
What do they see?

o o o

BIG IDEA / Others are always watching us to see how we respond to wins and losses; to success and failure. In times of disruption, what they see will determine how they perceive us. What are others observing about you?

READ / Chapter 1 in *The Sequence to Success*

○ ○ ○

RESPOND /

Why do you think disruption leads to more significant observations of others?

_____

_____

_____

_____

Have you ever discovered something about someone close to you during a time of disruption? How did this change your view of that person?

_____

_____

_____

_____

What have you discovered about yourself during times of hardship (whether positive or negative)?

_____

_____

_____

_____

○ ○ ○

REFLECT AND DISCUSS /

"The observations made during times of disruption are much more significant than those during seasons of peace, success, and harmony."

○ ○ ○

RESPOND /

Getting "big" or "little" refers to how we respond to hardship. Do you tend to try to make yourself bigger when conflict arises, or smaller? Why do you think this is?

_____

_____

_____

_____

_____

_____

_____

_____

_____

_____

How can even getting "smaller" cause others to lose respect for us?

_____

_____

_____

_____

_____

_____

_____

_____

_____

_____

_____

○ ○ ○

REFLECT AND DISCUSS /

"Do people notice if we're getting big or getting little? Of course they do! The people around us may be intimidated when we're loud and demanding. On the other hand, they may feel sorry for us when we've gotten so meek that we've almost vanished. However, either way, we lose their respect."

○ ○ ○

REFLECT AND DISCUSS /

"I'm always aware that first impressions are often lasting impressions, so it's important for me to set a positive tone in every encounter."

○ ○ ○

RESPOND /

What stands out to you about the story of the receptionist?

_____

_____

_____

_____

_____

_____

How do you practically go about making a good first impression with others?

_____

_____

_____

_____

_____

_____

What role does preparation play in making a good first impression? How can lack of preparation handicap your ability to do so?

_____

_____

_____

_____

_____

_____

RESPOND /

What practical steps can you take to understand your audience before you share your content?

_____

_____

_____

_____

_____

_____

_____

_____

Can you think of any speakers who communicated that they truly understood you as the audience? How did this make them more effective?

_____

_____

_____

_____

_____

_____

_____

_____

_____

○ ○ ○

REFLECT AND DISCUSS /

"Communication is as much art as science. We need to understand our audience, even if it's an audience of one."

PART 1 / Observations

CHAPTER 2

Better Lenses
When we look at others, what do we see?

○ ○ ○

BIG IDEA / Our upbringing and background greatly influences our first impressions of others. What we see springs from who we are. In an organizational sense, we must intentionally guide our focus by determining the "what" and "why" of everything we do.

○ ○ ○

READ / Chapter 2 in *The Sequence to Success*

○ ○ ○

REFLECT AND DISCUSS /

"We make the most accurate observations about people when we see them respond to stress. As leaders, parents, and friends, perhaps our greatest responsibility is to be students of people, to notice their character when they're under pressure and see how they use their intellect and talents to solve problems."

○ ○ ○

RESPOND /

What kinds of practical things can you do to become a student of other people?

_____

_____

_____

_____

When you've observed people out in public— either staff, customers, or passersby—in stressful situations, what indications of stress stand out to you?

_____

_____

_____

_____

Can you think of any indications that others might notice in *you* when you're stressed?

_____

_____

_____

How might we benefit from *not* immediately solving someone else's stress actually help both of you learn and grow?

_____

_____

_____

RESPOND /

Can you think of one way that your upbringing, or previous experiences, affects the way you perceive others?

_____

_____

_____

_____

_____

What are some of the first things you notice about new people when you meet or encounter them? Why do you think that is?

_____

_____

_____

_____

_____

Sometimes our intuition can alert us to dangerous individuals or situations. Can you recall a time that your "sixth sense" told you that something was off?

_____

_____

_____

_____

_____

○ ○ ○

REFLECT AND DISCUSS /

"All of our observations are colored by previous experiences, which serve as a grid upon which we put what we see about people and events."

RESPOND /

In your own words, what is the difference between someone's "what" and their "why"?

_____

_____

_____

_____

_____

_____

Why is it important to clearly define both of these aspects of your direction and vision?

_____

_____

_____

_____

_____

Right now, what is the main "what" in your life personally? What is your main "why"? How do they intersect?

_____

_____

_____

_____

_____

_____

○ ○ ○

REFLECT AND DISCUSS /

"Two organizations may have the same goal (their _what_), but they can have very different reasons for accomplishing it (their _why_)."

○ ○ ○

REFLECT AND DISCUSS /

"To some degree, most of us are plagued by *confirmation bias*— that is, we look for and listen to only the information that confirms what we already believe. In other words, we're not very open to differing opinions."

○ ○ ○

RESPOND /

Do you find it easy or difficult, most of the time, to listen to someone share opinions that don't align with your own?

_____

_____

_____

_____

What's your typical emotional reaction to receiving feedback or critique? Why do you think that is?

_____

_____

_____

_____

_____

Why do you think one-on-one conversations are the best atmosphere for most people to give or receive honest, constructive feedback with one another?

_____

_____

_____

_____

Did anything stand out to you from the "Developing Skills of Observation" section?

_____

_____

_____

_____

PART 2 / Opinions

CHAPTER 3

The Product of Opinions

Your life has been shaped by others' opinions of you.

○ ○ ○

BIG IDEA / We often receive others' opinions defensively, and guard our own vehemently. This is because so much of our identity has become wrapped up the opinions or beliefs we hold that many people can't even tell the difference. When we realize that our opinions aren't who we are, however, we become more open to change, compromise, and accepting criticism.

READ / Chapter 3 in *The Sequence to Success*

REFLECT AND DISCUSS /

"The pronunciation of my name was the first time people in this country misunderstood me, but it wasn't the last."

RESPOND /

How does Sam's story about having to change the pronunciation of his last name make you feel? Why do you think he made the decision that he did?

_____

_____

_____

_____

What's one compromise you could make that would make your business and interactions with others more smooth and harmonious?

_____

_____

_____

_____

Sam's wedding story shows that there are certain things he would not compromise on (spending the rest of his life with Brenda). What's one stance or personal decision that you will not allow others to talk you out of?

_____

_____

_____

_____

○ ○ ○

REFLECT AND DISCUSS /

"God has made us relational creatures. We live and die by the opinions of those around us. The question is: whose opinion matters the most?"

○ ○ ○

RESPOND /

Who are the people whose opinions matter most to you?

_____

_____

_____

Who are those who hold your opinion in high regard?

_____

_____

_____

Why do you think God made us relational— what are some of the reasons that we need others' encouragement, affirmation, and even correction?

_____

_____

_____

_____

How do the positive opinions of others make you feel?

_____

_____

_____

How do the negative opinions of others make you feel?

_____

_____

_____

_____

REFLECT AND DISCUSS /

"[When we receive criticism,] We're tempted or compelled to be instantly defensive. Stop, take a deep breath, relax your face, and soften your tone of voice."

RESPOND /

Criticism isn't inherently damaging to us... why do you think most people tense up or become defensive? What's really going on underneath the surface?

_____

_____

_____

_____

_____

_____

_____

_____

_____

Can you recall a time that someone's criticism helped you become better, or improved the quality of your work?

_____

_____

_____

_____

_____

_____

_____

_____

_____

_____

_____

○ ○ ○

RESPOND /

How do you think our personal sense of self, or security, gets wrapped up in our opinions?

_____

_____

_____

_____

_____

_____

○ ○ ○

REFLECT AND DISCUSS /

"People cling to their cherished opinions if they believe their security is based on it, but if not, they are usually very open to new ideas."

If more people realized the difference between security and opinion, how do you think it would affect debates and discussions in workplaces, on social media, and in family settings?

_____

_____

_____

_____

_____

Why do you think Sam argues that others' opinions of you constitute your "brand"? Do you agree with this statement? Why or why not?

_____

_____

_____

_____

_____

_____

PART 2 / Opinions
CHAPTER 4

Your Opinion Matters
Our conclusions have incredible power to change lives.

○ ○ ○

BIG IDEA / We can easily sense when others value our ideas. It's important for our opinions to be accurate, respectful, and not skewed by our personal preferences. Often times, as we carefully evaluate the lens through which we see the world, we'll realize we actually have more opportunities and options than we ever thought possible.

READ / Chapter 4 in *The Sequence to Success*

REFLECT AND DISCUSS /

"The leader doesn't have to buy every idea that members of the team generate, but every idea needs to be valued."

RESPOND /

In your own words, what's the difference between valuing an idea and buying into an idea?

_____

_____

_____

_____

What physical, verbal, and emotional cues tell you that someone values your ideas?

_____

_____

_____

_____

_____

What signals tell you that a person does not value your ideas?

_____

_____

_____

_____

_____

RESPOND /

What are some of your personal preferences that might affect how you see, interpret, or think about others?

_____

_____

_____

_____

_____

_____

Can you think of any types of people (i.e. creative, detailed, etc.) that you may automatically dismiss or discount because of your preferences?

_____

_____

_____

_____

_____

Why do you think quiet people are often overlooked? Conversely, why do you think talkative or assertive people tend to garner the bulk of the responsibilities being handed out in group settings?

_____

_____

_____

_____

o o o

REFLECT AND DISCUSS /

"Our opinions of others need to be accurate, not skewed by our personal preferences."

RESPOND /

Can you recall a time when a change in circumstance allowed you to see more opportunities than you had seen before?

_____

_____

_____

_____

_____

_____

_____

Who are the people in your life who model good decision-making for you?

_____

_____

_____

_____

_____

For whom do you model good decision-making? Who looks up to you for guidance?

_____

_____

_____

_____

_____

REFLECT AND DISCUSS /

"We often have more options than we realize."

RESPOND /

What does Paul and John Mark's story have to teach us about forming opinions of others?

_____

_____

_____

_____

_____

_____

_____

_____

_____

_____

Can you think of any people towards whom your opinion has changed over the last 5, 10, or 15 years? What do you think caused this shift inside you?

_____

_____

_____

_____

_____

_____

_____

_____

_____

_____

REFLECT AND DISCUSS /

"We often have more options than we realize."

PART 3 / Opportunities
CHAPTER 5

The People Standing at Our Doors
They've given us opportunities.

o o o

BIG IDEA / The opportunities that others give to us is heavily determined by the observations they make about us. Many times, the way we receive their feedback and how respectful we are can directly influence what opportunities we walk into. It's so important to remain humble, grateful, and respectful as we grow into the leaders we were meant to become.

RESPOND /

Have you formed any new relationships
recently with people you trust and respect?

_____

_____

_____

○ ○ ○

REFLECT AND DISCUSS /

"It's all about
establishing
relationships
based on trust and
respect, and people
who benefit telling
their friends."

Where can you seek out connections with
those who run in similar circles to you?

_____

_____

_____

How can you make yourself more available for
those who would benefit from knowing you?

_____

_____

_____

_____

How can these close connections keep us
on the right road when we begin to veer off
course? Who in your life acts as an agent of
correction and accountability?

_____

_____

_____

REFLECT AND DISCUSS /

"Many leaders believe the only way to set the pace for their organizations is to be relentlessly positive, even when they feel deeply discouraged."

○ ○ ○

RESPOND /

What about work and leadership culture do you think creates this unrealistic expectation?

_____

_____

_____

_____

_____

_____

_____

Do you feel this pressure in your life currently? Is it difficult for you to admit when you're feeling exhausted, apathetic, or discouraged? Why do you think that is?

_____

_____

_____

_____

_____

_____

What's one practical way that leaders can begin normalize and mitigate the insecurities, fears, and limitations that all leaders experience?

_____

_____

_____

_____

_____

o o o

REFLECT AND DISCUSS /

"With courage, creativity, and tenacity, we can still walk through the doors of opportunity."

o o o

RESPOND /

Do you agree with Sam's argument that our mindset heavily dictates the opportunities we'll encounter? Why or why not?

_____

_____

_____

_____

_____

_____

What "hard work" might be in store for you as you prepare to walk into new doors of opportunity? What work are you already doing to prepare for this?

_____

_____

_____

_____

_____

The only part of the process we can control is others' observations of us. How does this narrowed focus actually empower us to improve our opportunities?

_____

_____

_____

_____

_____

RESPOND /

What are three practical ways in which you can show interest in those around you this week?

_____

_____

_____

_____

Why do you think so many people in our culture can't civilly disagree with one another?

_____

_____

_____

_____

In your opinion, what does it look like to disagree and still value the other person and their point of view?

_____

_____

_____

_____

Lastly, reflect on just a few of the people who have opened doors for you. List their names and how they helped you take that next step. Who do you need to call, text, email, or meet in person to say thank you?

_____

_____

_____

_____

○ ○ ○

REFLECT AND DISCUSS /

"We make the best impressions when we take the focus off ourselves and show genuine interest in the other person."

PART 3 / Opportunities

CHAPTER 6

Our Hands On Their Doors
*Providing opportunities for
the people around you.*

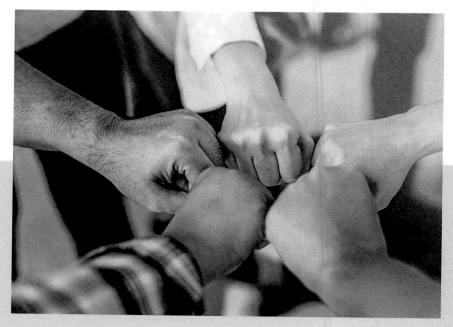

o o o

BIG IDEA / Personal connections and organizational connections hold immense potential, both for ourselves and for those around us. It all depends on how much responsibility we're willing to take for our own leadership. When we begin to lead with excellence, and to champion those around us, doors of opportunity will begin to open for everyone— it's a never-ending chain of transformation!

READ / Chapter 6 in *The Sequence to Success*

REFLECT AND DISCUSS /

"From the beginning, I observed Benson's powerfully positive impact on others. It didn't take long to develop a glowing opinion of him; over the years, this opinion grew even stronger."

RESPOND /

What does Sam's story about Benson have to show us about the process of observations, opinions, and opportunities?

_____

_____

_____

_____

Can you think of anyone in your life for whom you can open doors of opportunity? What positive characteristics in this person stand out to you?

_____

_____

_____

_____

How have others' words of life positively impacted you and your leadership?

_____

_____

_____

_____

What effect do negative words, or words of death, have on you and those around you?

_____

_____

_____

_____

○ ○ ○

REFLECT AND DISCUSS /

"The biggest impact we can have on others is through authentic personal connections."

○ ○ ○

RESPOND /

Why do you think the greatest impact is found in personal connections, instead of organizational or occupational connections?

_____

_____

_____

_____

_____

Conversely, what opportunities and benefits can you think of that are available in the organizational world, but aren't always available in personal connections?

_____

_____

_____

_____

_____

In your own opinion, why is it essential to win over people's hearts before recruiting their heads and hands?

_____

_____

_____

_____

_____

REFLECT AND DISCUSS /

"In fact, the failure to take responsibility for failure and the failure to recognize the contributions of others are two of the most serious leadership flaws."

o o o

RESPOND /

How do leaders practically fail to take responsibility? In other words, how can you tell when a leader is blame-shifting and shirking responsibility?

_____

_____

_____

_____

_____

Can you recall a time when you failed to recognize the contributions of others? How do you think that affected this person?

_____

_____

_____

_____

What about when your personal contributions weren't recognized or fully appreciated? How did this make you feel?

_____

_____

_____

_____

Did any of Sam's points stand out to you in the "Teach People to Look For Opportunities" section?

_____

_____

_____

_____

RESPOND /

In your opinion, what does it look like when a leader "multiplies" himself or herself?

_____

_____

_____

_____

_____

_____

_____

What are two or three practical steps you can take to start multiplying yourself?

_____

_____

_____

_____

_____

_____

Who can you brag about this week? What good qualities or contributions can you praise in that person?

_____

_____

_____

_____

_____

_____

○ ○ ○

REFLECT AND DISCUSS /

"A very effective leader multiplies himself throughout the leadership team."

CONCLUSION

○ ○ ○

READ / Conclusion *The Sequence to Success*

○ ○ ○

REFLECT AND DISCUSS /

"As our observations become more astute, our opinions of people will be more accurate and we can tailor our communication appropriately about the next steps of opportunity."

○ ○ ○

RESPOND /

What's one impactful lesson from this study that you'll take with you as you grow in your leadership?

_____

_____

_____

_____

_____

_____

Who is one person you can share this study with who can also benefit from it?

_____

_____

_____

_____

In one sentence, how can you improve in your efforts to provide opportunities to others?

_____

_____

_____

_____

_____

_____

RESPOND /

Which of the five bullets Sam presents stands out to you most? Why do you think it caught your eye?

_____

_____

_____

_____

_____

_____

_____

_____

_____

_____

_____

How can you integrate this practice into your leadership?

_____

_____

_____

_____

_____

_____

_____

_____

_____

○ ○ ○

REFLECT AND DISCUSS /

"In my role as a consultant and in your role as a leader, spouse, parent, or friend, we can become more proficient in five consecutive abilities."

○ ○ ○

REFLECT AND DISCUSS /

"As our eyes are opened to see Him more as He really is, we change from the inside out. This is the most important observation in our lives and we need to get it right."

○ ○ ○

RESPOND /

Why is our observation about God more influential in our lives than any other?

_____

_____

_____

_____

What are just a few of your observations about God?

_____

_____

_____

_____

How do you think your upbringing, culture, and family have impacted your views on who God is? Have your views deviated at all from what your upbringing taught you?

_____

_____

_____

_____

_____

Are there any other closing thoughts, actions steps, or reflections on your mind as you end this study?

_____

_____

_____

_____

NOTES